C16.3

000115396

D0445294

DISCARD

DRUG DANGERS

DIET PILL
DRUG DANGERS

Lawrence Clayton, Ph.D.

Enslow Publishers, Inc.

44 Fadem Road   PO Box 38
Box 699   Aldershot
Springfield, NJ 07081   Hants GU12 6BP
USA   UK

http://www.enslow.com

To the Roddy family:
Ron, Shirley, Jeremy, and Rob

Library of Congress Cataloging-in-Publication Data

Clayton, L. (Lawrence)
     Diet pill drug dangers / Lawrence Clayton.
          p.   cm. — (Drug dangers)
     Includes bibliographical references and index.
     Summary: Examines the history of diet pill use, focusing on
society's obsession with weight loss and the dangers of abusing
these drugs.
     ISBN 0-7660-1158-5
     1. Appetite depressants—Health aspects—Juvenile literature.
[1. Appetite depressants. 2. Drug abuse.] I. Title. II. Series.
RM332.3.C53   1999
616.3'98061–dc21   98-20514
                                                                         CIP
                                                                          AC

Printed in the United States of America

10 9 8 7 6 5 4 3 2 1

To Our Readers:
All Internet addresses in this book were active and appropriate when
we went to press. Any comments or suggestions can be sent by e-mail
to Comments@enslow.com or to the address on the back cover.

Photo Credits: Corel Corporation, pp. 9, 11, 20, 25, 27, 38, 39; Díamar
Interactive Corp., pp. 45, 48, 51, 52; National Archives, pp. 15, 32.

Cover Photo: Corel Corporation

contents

one

Diet Pills: New Questions, Same Answers

This is the story of "Jean's" (not her real name) problems with diet pills, as told to the author. [1]

"It seems to me that I've always had a weight problem. As a child, I was bigger than other kids my age. It wasn't until junior high that I really became aware of the difference that made and would make in my life.

"That year everybody was talking about how beautiful Julia Roberts looked in the movie *Pretty Woman*. We all tried to dress and talk like her. I remember my best friend and I trying to find boots like Julia's—going to store after store at the mall. We did find cute polka-dot dresses like the one Julia wore to the polo match. Jan's looked great on her, but she was tall and slim. I was short and dumpy. Needless to say, mine looked terrible on me. Jan was looking at herself in the mirror and smiling from ear to ear. Then, she turned to look at me, and her smile vanished. I could feel the tears starting to brim in my eyes. Jan turned red and looked away. She said, "I can't afford this. Let's go get some ice cream." I know she was trying to be nice, but I'll never forget that look.

"From then on, I hated my body. I tried everything I could think of to lose weight. Nothing worked. My parents are both overweight and so are all of my aunts and uncles. One of my cousins died of heart failure when he was fourteen. The doctor said it was because of being so overweight. I guess I was just born to be fat.

"Once, in high school, a boy insulted me in front of the whole class. I was taking home economics, and I had learned to sew. It was one of the few things I was really good at. I worked very hard to make an outfit for "dress-up day." I was so proud of myself when I walked into class that day. Then one of the boys said I looked like I was wearing a tent. I ran to the bathroom and refused to go back to class. They finally had to call my father to come and pick me up.

"My life is like that—one continual embarrassment over my weight. No one ever wanted me on their team. If they had to choose up sides, I was always the last one chosen. It was like that in dating, too. No one ever wanted me. If I even smiled at a boy, he would look away.

"I guess after that, I kind of retreated into a fantasy world. I read every romance novel I could get my hands on. In my mind, I was the heroine—the raving beauty who was just too irresistible to turn away from. Inside, I was dying.

"I was sixteen the first time I tried to kill myself. Everyone was getting ready for the prom. I was desperate to go. I had such a crush on a boy named Danny that I thought I would die. Of course, he did not ask me to the prom. He asked one of the other girls. That night I swallowed a whole bottle of aspirin. But they just made me sick and I threw them all up. I was in the kitchen, and my mother saw them.

"She made an appointment for me with the doctor. I had made up my mind that I would not tell him anything, but two days later, I sat in his office and blubbered out the whole story. He started me on a diet drug called fenfluramine. It worked like a charm. I lost all of the weight I needed to loose. Then I started increasing the number of pills I was taking.

"In October, I got sick. Breathing was very difficult. I

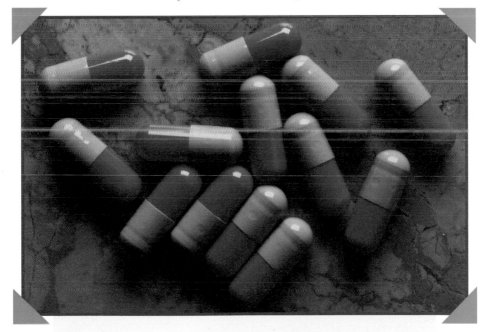

When they are taken as prescribed, under the supervision of a doctor, diet pills can be quite effective. However, as is true of any drug, side effects are always possible. If the side effects are severe, the user could develop serious health problems with continued use of diet pills.

couldn't seem to get enough air. The doctor said I had developed side effects from the diet pills. He said I should quit taking them for a while. I guess I really threw a fit. I screamed and begged. But he just said, 'No more.' I cried all the way home.

"During the next several weeks, I got more and more depressed. I couldn't do anything. All I did was sit in my room and cry. I guess I just lost control, because I couldn't quit. And I had a terrible headache—the worst I've ever had. It just went on and on, day after day. It was so bad, it hurt when I moved my eyes. The doctor gave me something for the headache, but the depression got worse. I couldn't sleep at all.

"The holidays were the worst time for me. Now that school was out, there was nothing to take my mind off my problems. The depression just did me in. All I could think of was killing myself. I just wanted to be dead. Although I had never been much of a drinker, I started raiding my father's bar. I got drunk almost every day—while my parents were at work.

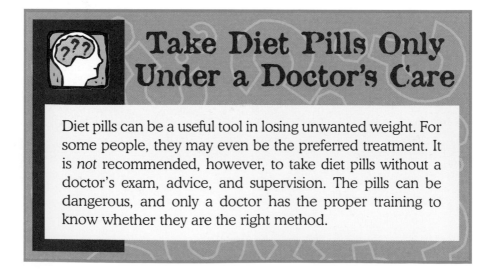

Take Diet Pills Only Under a Doctor's Care

Diet pills can be a useful tool in losing unwanted weight. For some people, they may even be the preferred treatment. It is *not* recommended, however, to take diet pills without a doctor's exam, advice, and supervision. The pills can be dangerous, and only a doctor has the proper training to know whether they are the right method.

Many teens believe that in order to be popular or successful, they must look like models.

"I was in the hospital for thirty-four days. At first, they kept me drugged up. But little by little they forced me to open up. I finally realized that people did love me—my parents, teachers, and friends. I was released on Valentine's Day. When I got home, my parents and friends had decorated my room with flowers. I still don't have much energy. I also have chest pain and get short of breath. My doctor can't tell me exactly when or if I'll ever get better."

The extent of problems that young people have with weight and diet pills was underscored by a news release from the Centers for Disease Control. It stated that one in six children between the eighth and tenth grade had tried diet pills.[2] A study from the University of California stated: "By eleven years of age, 80 percent were dieting: by eighteen years of age, 100 percent had used some extreme method to control their weight."[3]

two

Teens and Self-Image

One of the big issues in being popular is appearance. A look at copies of *YM*, a popular magazine for young women, shows just how important personal appearance is. Virtually every issue has at least one article dealing with personal appearance. So does *Seventeen*, another popular magazine for young women.

Unfortunately, in today's world, looking good often means being slim—sometimes too slim—so slim it can be dangerous. Take "Alexandria" (not her real name) of Fort Worth, Texas.[1]

When Alexandria was little, she used to pretend that she was a model. She and her friends would dress up in their mothers' clothes. They would take turns walking up and down the sidewalk like the models and beauty queens they saw on television. Alexandria was very proud of her slim figure and small hips. In her mind's eye, she was the next Miss America. When she got older, she would be a Dallas Cowboys cheerleader. Then, it was on to Hollywood.

But when she was twelve, her body started to change. Her hips were wider, and she was getting curves where she didn't want them. She was also putting on weight. She didn't look like the models she saw on television anymore. Instead, she thought she looked more and more like a defensive lineman for a football team. That's when she heard about Mini Thins™ diet pills. A friend said she could buy them at the convenience store near school. Several of her friends were using them, and it seemed like an easy way to get her figure back. Maybe she could become a model after all.

Alexandria loved the way the pills made her feel. She had twice the energy and a lot more confidence. In two weeks, she lost five pounds. But was that enough?

She decided that losing five more pounds would not hurt. That was thirty pounds ago. When the stores stopped carrying Mini Thins, Alexandria did not know what she would do. She felt terrible, and she was putting on weight.

About that time, another friend suggested that she try a street drug called speed. Her friend said it worked the same way the diet pills did. Alexandria was desperate, so she tried it. She used speed for two months before she admitted that she might be addicted.

We live in a society that places excessive value on being thin. The signs of that are everywhere. It's not just *YM* and *Seventeen* that contain articles about these topics. So do adult magazines such as *McCall's*,[2] *Family Circle*,[3] and *Cosmopolitan*.[4]

A recent *Sally Jessie Raphael* show was about the

Speed, the street name for a drug called methamphetamine, is a highly addictive drug, that is sometimes used by people who think that they can control or solve weight problems. Unfortunately, speed creates more problems than it solves.

experiences of adolescents who were repeatedly abused by their peers because of being overweight.[5] It was called, "I Just Want to Be Pretty." Her guests were Randi, Crystal, Marlene, and Renay.

Renay said that she spent most of her time at school being tormented by other students. She referred to school experience as "one continuous nightmare." Once when she was in the rest room, girls grabbed her and washed out her eyes with soap for looking at them. They called her "ugly" and said that she was garbage. They used to sing "Renay has fleas" in music class. On the bus, they would punch her in the stomach and refuse to sit by her.

Marlene also reported that other students, both boys and girls, were rude to her in junior high school. They made her click her heels together, then scolded her because she had not gone home instantly like Dorothy in *The Wizard of Oz*. She went home crying many times. Once, the other girls paid a boy to ask her out in front of the whole lunchroom. Then, they laughed at her. These same girls continued their abuse in high school. For a long time, Marlene tried to avoid them by not going to school, averaging only two days' attendance a week. At age twenty-one, she claimed that she would never get over feeling ugly. When she did start dating a guy, she always got horribly jealous because she did not believe that she could measure up to others.

Crystal was just thirteen when she appeared on the *Sally Jesse Raphael* show. She is a special education student. Peers said she was fat and called her names. They sometimes barked at her. Every morning, her mother would fix her hair. On the bus, the other girls pulled it until it was a mess. Her mother, Hope, was also on the show. She reported the other kids' behavior to the school and was told that there was nothing that could be done—after all, they were just kids. During the past year, Crystal dieted and lost all of her excess weight. Her mother bought her a whole new outfit. The girls still came up to their house, stood on the porch, called Crystal names, and barked. Crystal asked to switch schools. So far, her request has been denied.

Some of the guests on the show had become desperate. Randi had tried plastic surgery—a tummy tuck and breast reduction. She also tried liposuction. Karen was fired from her job because she believed others were looking at her—and she told her boss. She was afraid she would never have a normal life.

Nancy Friday, author of *The Power of Beauty*, said, "Today, we prize looks more than anything. Beauty is what gets you attention, gets you served, and gets you loved."[6] As we have seen, being thin has a lot to do with how others conceive of beauty.

Eating Disorders

Many young people are so obsessed with being thin that they develop eating disorders such as anorexia nervosa (in which a person starves themselves) or bulimia (eating then forcing oneself to vomit or using some other method to get the food out of the body). Along with these disorders young people often abuse diet pills.

Anorexia. Lots of young people, as many as 10 percent, have some problems with anorexia.[7] Many others go on extended crash diets. This makes it difficult for parents and others to decide whether someone suffers from an eating disorder. Martha Everett, at sixteen, did just that. Her story appeared in *Seventeen* and was entitled "Dying to Be Thin."[8]

It all started when she was thirteen. She was at summer camp and worried about getting her period. She had heard that strict dieting could put it off for a while. So, she began restricting her foods to fruit and salads. Over the summer she lost three pounds and became obsessed with food and being thin.

Soon she started an extensive exercise program. She continued to lose weight. She became so malnourished that she did not have the energy to do her schoolwork. By the time she was fourteen, she was five feet two inches tall, weighed sixty-nine pounds, and was so sick that she had to be admitted to a hospital.

Bulimia. Many people try to control their weight by eating excessively, then vomiting, using laxatives, diuretics, or diet pills. This condition is called bulimia. Studies show that about 20 percent of women under twenty years of age have used vomiting as a means of weight control.

"Emilee," (not her real name) age fourteen, was not happy with her body.[10] One of the boys at school had called her "chubby." She stood looking in the mirror in

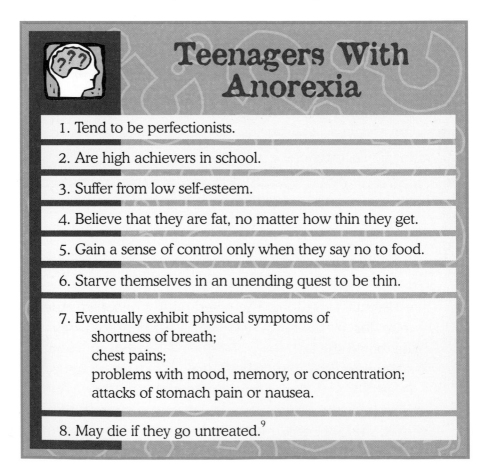

Teenagers With Anorexia

1. Tend to be perfectionists.

2. Are high achievers in school.

3. Suffer from low self-esteem.

4. Believe that they are fat, no matter how thin they get.

5. Gain a sense of control only when they say no to food.

6. Starve themselves in an unending quest to be thin.

7. Eventually exhibit physical symptoms of
shortness of breath;
chest pains;
problems with mood, memory, or concentration;
attacks of stomach pain or nausea.

8. May die if they go untreated.[9]

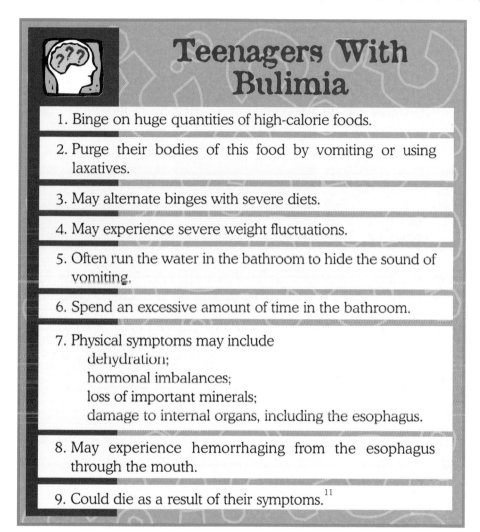

Teenagers With Bulimia

1. Binge on huge quantities of high-calorie foods.

2. Purge their bodies of this food by vomiting or using laxatives.

3. May alternate binges with severe diets.

4. May experience severe weight fluctuations.

5. Often run the water in the bathroom to hide the sound of vomiting.

6. Spend an excessive amount of time in the bathroom.

7. Physical symptoms may include
   dehydration;
   hormonal imbalances;
   loss of important minerals;
   damage to internal organs, including the esophagus.

8. May experience hemorrhaging from the esophagus through the mouth.

9. Could die as a result of their symptoms.[11]

her parents' bathroom. She hated how she looked. And tryouts for the cheerleading squad were in two days. What could she do?

Moments later she found herself in an eating frenzy. She ate six doughnuts, a huge bowl of ice cream, five Popsicles™, and a candy bar. She was miserable. She wished she had not eaten that first doughnut. She felt sick to her stomach.

Bulimics will binge on large quantities of high-calorie foods, such as cookies and candy. They get the food out of their system by vomiting, by using laxatives, or by using water pills.

She went into the bathroom, bent over the toilet bowl, stuck her fingers down her throat, and vomited. When she was through, she wiped her mouth with a rag. Then, she took two of her mother's diuretics (water pills), five laxative tablets, three diet pills, and drank four glasses of water.

By tomorrow evening, she would be ready for the tryouts. And she was, but this coping strategy turned into a habit. Whenever she was under stress or worried about something, she went on a food binge. Then, she vomited and took laxatives, diuretics, and diet pills.

By the time she was fifteen, Emilee was in trouble. She had begun to vomit blood. Doctors told her that repeated exposure to stomach acid had damaged her esophagus (the tube that runs from the mouth to the stomach). And her blood pressure was extremely high from using diet pills.

Obsessive Overeating. Compulsive (uncontrollable) overeating is another type of eating disorder. People with this problem eat even when they are not hungry. They usually eat because of some emotional need. They may be anxious, angry, depressed, or lonely. In other words, they eat for the wrong reasons.

These people often gain huge amounts of weight. The weight gain then makes them more emotionally distressed. Some people become so depressed over their weight that they do not want to live.

Kathy Trustman was one such person.[12] She became obsessed with food. This started after a bout with anorexia during high school.

Kathy said she got mixed messages—food was good

Yo-Yo Syndrome

Many obsessive eaters try to compensate for overeating by using diet pills. This often results in weight loss. When they are successful, they feel wonderful. Eventually, however, they begin overeating again. This causes them to put the weight right back on. Then, they feel terrible and start using diet pills again. This is known as the "Yo-Yo Syndrome," because their weight goes up and down like a yo-yo.

Those who stay on this cycle may damage their health. Each time they lose weight, they lose both muscle and fat. Each time they gain the weight back, it is mostly fat.

for you, and it was bad for you. This caused her to eat excessively, but to feel guilty about it.

This type of behavior is typical of obsessive overeaters. They often feel good when they eat and bad after they eat. Then they eat even more because it makes them feel good again. But, of course, they feel guilty about that, and. . . . It is a never-ending cycle.

To make matters worse, each time they diet, they lose some muscle tissue, and each time they gain weight, they gain fat. This means that the more times the diet pills work, the fatter they will become.

The only way to avoid this is to lose weight and keep it off. This can only be achieved through a change in lifestyle that includes permanently staying on a healthy diet and a good exercise program. These things will be discussed in detail in Chapter 6.

three

Confessions of a Diet Pill Addict

This chapter tells the story of the impact diet pills had on the life of a person who started using these medications because of a weight problem and ended up addicted to them.[1] Her story seems to be fairly typical of diet pill addicts.

When did you first become aware that you had a weight problem?

"I think it was at about the age of twelve. I noticed that I was bigger than other girls my age. I wasn't really fat, just bigger—'pleasantly plump,' my dad used to say.

"I think what first started bothering me is that I couldn't wear the styles the other girls wore. I wanted to have cool clothes like my friends.

"Most adults don't understand how important fitting in is to a girl that age. All my friends were getting their figures, and so was I. But mine didn't look like theirs did. There was just too much of me. I became absolutely desperate to fit in, to be smaller."

Did people put pressure on you to lose weight?
"Not directly. I mean nobody said, 'You are too fat,' or 'You're repulsive,' or anything like that. But there are lots of ways people put subtle pressure on you. Boys don't look at you the same way they look at the slimmer girls, and they don't tease you the same way either. You get the message that you're not OK, and you know it is because of your weight.

"This has quite an impact on your self-image. When I was younger, I was pretty athletic. And I participated in all kinds of sports. As my self-image and confidence took a nosedive, I stopped. I didn't want other people watching me. I became more and more self-conscious. I began to withdraw from various activities—and from other people. I guess I isolated myself as a way of protecting myself."

Did you try to do anything about your weight?
"Lots of things."

Like what?
"First, I cut back on sweets. That didn't help at all. I was still bigger than my friends. I hated the way I looked. So, I started dieting. I'd lose a few pounds, but never enough. My mother said I was 'big-boned,' but I knew the truth. I was fat, and I was determined to do something about it.

"After that I tried everything. I tried the Cambridge™ diet. It was very effective. I lost all the weight I wanted. I was so happy. My mother bought me a few new outfits, and boys were noticing me. Of course, as soon as I started eating normal foods again, I gained it all back—

and more. I kept those outfits for years, always hoping to be able to fit into them again.

"Next I tried Slim Fast™. It worked, too, but we didn't have the money for me to stay on it.

"That's when I got into all the fad diets. I tried the Grapefruit Diet, the Tomato and Egg Diet, and the Pineapple Diet. I guess I tried every diet I could find. I even tried the Body-Type Diet.

What is the Body-Type Diet?
"It was designed for people with different types of bodies. Some people just put on weight above the waist, others just on their trunks. Me, I put mine on my hips and legs. On the Body Type Diet, you had special foods that were

Fad diets such as the Tomato and Egg Diet, the Pineapple Diet, and the Grapefruit Diet may seem effective at first. But, like any other diet, they actually change the way your body breaks down fat. In the long run, the dieter will actually gain weight.

supposed to be more effective for people with your body type.

"I know it sounds silly, but it actually worked for me. I lost a lot of weight on it. I could almost get into those outfits again, but I was older and just too big, despite the fact that I was pretty trim. Of course, I gained all my weight back.

"I remember standing on the scale. I weighed 150 pounds. I went to my closet and took down those outfits and threw them in the trash. Then I went to the bathroom and just stood there looking in the mirror and cried. I was so miserable. That was the first time I wished I could die."

Did you try to harm yourself?
"No."

What stopped you?
"I always had faith that God would help me somehow. I just knew that he wouldn't leave me like that. So, I started to pray for his help.

"A couple of weeks later, I heard about a doctor who was helping people lose weight. I believed that he was the answer to my prayers."

What did you do?
"I called his office and found out how much it cost. The nurse told me it was 135 dollars to get started and 70 dollars a month after that. I knew my parents could never afford that. But I was desperate. So, I got a job at a hamburger place after school and saved the money. And I kept pestering my mother until she took me.

"First, they did a bunch of tests. Then, they put me on vitamins and a drug called phentermine. It was very

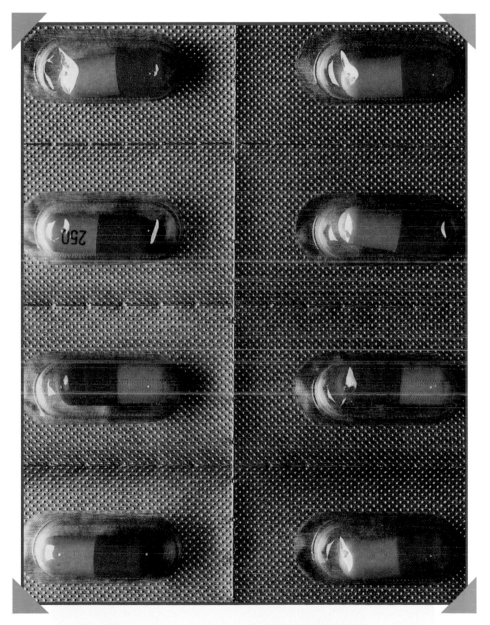

Looking for a quick, magical remedy to weight problems, some young people will abuse over-the-counter diet pills.

effective. I lost a lot of weight, and I had more energy than I had ever had. I used to run home from school, change clothes, go to work, come home at 10:00 P.M., and do homework until 1:00 or 2:00 A.M. I almost never slept.

"I don't remember exactly when I started doubling up on the dosage. But I remember that after a while, it just wasn't as effective. I would make up excuses to get the doctor to give me more."

What kinds of excuses?

"Oh, things like, 'My mother cleaned up my room and threw them out,' and 'I lost them at school.' Once I told him that I accidentally dropped the bottle in the toilet. I could tell he was starting to get suspicious.

"Before anything came down on that, my dad got a job and we moved halfway across the state. In the new place, I couldn't find a job, so I didn't have the money to go to a new weight doctor. That was a terrible time for me. I got so depressed. All I wanted to do was sleep. I got so far behind with my homework that school was a nightmare. I didn't know what was wrong back then. Now I realize that I was in withdrawal. My body and mind had gotten used to the diet pills, and I needed them to function. Of course, I put back on all the weight I had lost, and more."

Did you try anything else?

"Oh, yes! I finally got enough money together to go to another weight loss center. But the doctor didn't prescribe phentermine. She told me about a new drug that she felt was even more effective and had none of the side effects. It was called fenfluramine. Despite the fact that I was skeptical, I agreed to give it a try.

"Once again, I lost weight, but this time it was different. I felt kind of sick most of the time. I kept complaining about it, but I think the doctor just thought I wanted more phentermine."

Did you?
"Actually, I did. But she wouldn't hear of it. So I just kept complaining. Then, on one of my visits, she told me about a new medicine, which she said worked even better. It was called dexfenfluramine. She said some doctors were using it together with phentermine and having fantastic results.

"I said I'd like to try it. Man, did I lose the weight! I got down to 106 and was a size 7. I hadn't been that small since I was in the eighth grade.

"But that was the beginning of the end for me."

What do you mean "the beginning of the end?"
"I started getting really sick. I was having a lot of pain on the left side of my chest. And I was having trouble breathing. Last spring, I had to be taken to the emergency room in an ambulance. I was in the hospital for three weeks, two in intensive care. They said I was going into a coma. All I remembered was being able to see, but not being able to feel anything.

"Eventually, my lungs did clear up and I was able to go home. But I had to drop out of school. I was just too far behind and too tired to do anything about it. I would not finish until three years after the rest of my class had graduated."

How are you feeling now?
"Not good. I'm exhausted three days out of four. My chest still hurts all the time, and my pulse and blood pressure

are very irregular. I have some problems with my memory, and I can't concentrate. I still have problems with fluid in my lungs because my heart doesn't work right. That makes breathing difficult. My doctor says it's from having chronic high blood pressure, which is a side effect of the diet pills.

"And I've put all my weight back on again. Some days I'm so depressed I just sit and stare."

four

How Diet Pills Work

Being overweight in today's society can be a painful experience. Those who are overweight long for a solution to their problems. They diet, exercise, and consult physicians in their quest to lose weight. Sometimes the physicians choose to treat these people with diet pills.

Some people abuse these medications by taking more than their doctors tell them to take. Some abuse over-the-counter diet pills. Others buy illegal drugs. Too many people are looking for some magic solution to their weight problems.

People who begin to abuse diet pills usually have no idea how these chemicals will affect the mind and body. They also do not understand that taking diet pills will impact the way they think and act.

The oldest and most frequently abused class of diet pills are known as amphetamines and

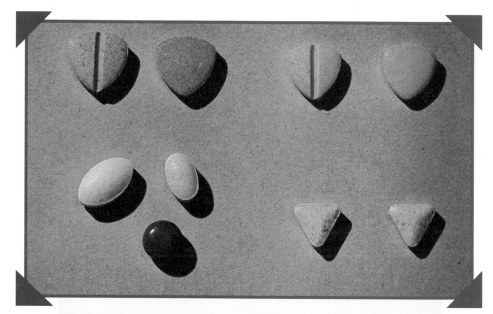

Methamphetamines, often prescribed by doctors for weight control, speed up the user's body and brain. It is this effect that earned the drug its street name—speed.

methamphetamines. They work by speeding up the user's body and brain. In fact, that is how methamphetamine got its street name—speed. It speeds up everything. Research shows that 80 percent of all stimulants are prescribed for weight control.[1]

Unfortunately, these medications cause many unwanted problems (called side effects) that affect the body and the brain. In addition, they may interact with other medications people take in ways that range from unpleasant to fatal.

Physical Effects

Amphetamines speed up the heart, making it pound as it pumps the blood through the body. This pounding of the heart dramatically increases the blood pressure, and makes stroke and heart attack more likely.

It also speeds up the lungs, causing breathing to become difficult as if the person were recovering from running a race. Users have a chronically dry mouth and increase the chance that the lungs will put too much oxygen into the bloodstream.

The user then flushes or turns red as if they were suddenly embarrassed. They may experience dizziness from too much oxygen in their brains, and they may have severe headaches.

These drugs also increase the gastric juices in the stomach. As a result, users often develop a nervous stomach. They may feel nauseous, and have stomach cramps, diarrhea, and increased urination. Some vomit frequently. Under these conditions, almost everyone experiences a loss of appetite. Most users complain that they have muscle tremors throughout the body and involuntary twitching of the legs and arms. These drugs even speed up the sweat glands. This causes some users to perspire heavily and to develop a rash. In some people, the rash can be fairly severe, becoming a horribly disfiguring form of acne nicknamed "speed bumps."

One of the problems of this type of diet pill is physical addiction. If a person uses these drugs long enough, the body will eventually begin to adjust to them. Once that happens, it is nearly impossible to quit. Those who try to quit often find that their bodies just will not function properly without the drug.

Emotional Effects

Amphetamine and methamphetamine diet pills do not just speed up the body. They also speed up the mind. This

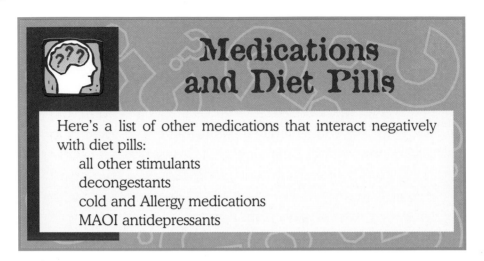

Medications and Diet Pills

Here's a list of other medications that interact negatively with diet pills:

all other stimulants

decongestants

cold and Allergy medications

MAOI antidepressants

process causes users to have a stream of thoughts. Some people become overwhelmed and have trouble concentrating. Others will become overanxious and may have panic attacks.

They may feel so restless and nervous that they have difficulty sleeping. When they do sleep, they have frightening dreams. Abusers may also become angry and irritable. For some, this will result in their becoming so violent that they seriously harm others.

For those who have been using diet pills for an extended period, the risk of psychological addiction is very high. Addiction is especially possible for those who have not been taking them as their doctor ordered. They get used to thinking too quickly, having excess mental energy, and going without sleep. (With psychological addiction the user becomes addicted to the feelings associated with diet pill use.)

When they try to quit, users become sluggish and sleep excessively. They also become horribly depressed— so depressed that they may become suicidal. These reactions to stopping the use of diet pills are an indication that the person is psychologically dependent. They will need to seek professional help to safely stop taking diet pills.[2]

Those who become addicted are in continual emotional pain. They may begin to develop strategies to shield themselves from that pain. Psychologists call these strategies defenses. One of the most-used defenses is denial. This defense enables the addict to believe that he or she is not addicted to the drug.

Another defense is the repression of feelings. This defense causes addicts to have little or no experience of pain. In a sense, they are hiding the pain—from themselves. They also hide their feelings from others, causing a loss of intimacy.

One of the few feelings that addicts express is anger. This causes them to blame everyone else for their problem—their doctor, their parents, their teachers, whoever is handy. In this way, they can avoid responsibility for their continued drug abuse. It also drives others away.

Drug Interactions

Diet pills often react negatively with other medications a person may be taking. In fact, the *Physicians' Desk Reference* warns doctors against prescribing diet pills to patients who are currently taking medication for depression, heart problems, pain, cough, colds, or blood pressure problems.[3]

Remember, never take these medications if you drink alcohol, smoke cigarettes, use caffeine products, or take other stimulants.

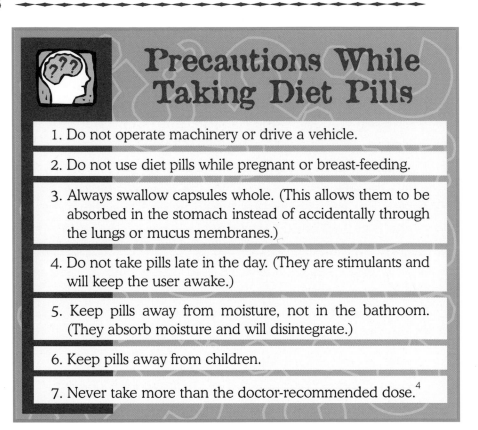

Precautions While Taking Diet Pills

1. Do not operate machinery or drive a vehicle.

2. Do not use diet pills while pregnant or breast-feeding.

3. Always swallow capsules whole. (This allows them to be absorbed in the stomach instead of accidentally through the lungs or mucus membranes.)

4. Do not take pills late in the day. (They are stimulants and will keep the user awake.)

5. Keep pills away from moisture, not in the bathroom. (They absorb moisture and will disintegrate.)

6. Keep pills away from children.

7. Never take more than the doctor-recommended dose.[4]

The New Diet Pills

In 1992, researchers discovered that two diet medications, prescribed together, seemed to be highly effective in controlling appetite. These medications were named fenfluramine and phentermine (known as fen-phen)[5]. Each of these diet pills taken alone had many side effects. But for some reason, the side effects seemed to disappear when the two drugs were taken together. This new combination appeared to be relatively safe to use. It also did not seem to be addictive.

Many people thought this combination of medications was the answer to the problems the other pills caused. Articles appeared in major magazines, proclaiming a "Better Way: The New (Doctor Approved) Diet Pills,"[6] and asking readers, "Could This Pill Be What You're Hungry For?"[7]

Patients thought these new medications were wonderful, almost miraculous. They could use them without any problems and for as long as they wanted. Many people who had never been able to lose weight did so for the first time. No one could have possibly foreseen the problems that were about to surface.

In 1996, a woman complaining of shortness of breath was admitted to the Mayo Clinic in Rochester, New York.[8] The doctors determined that she needed heart surgery. When they operated, they found a white, shiny, waxy material in her heart. The white substance was stopping the valves of her heart from working properly. This was the kind of thing doctors would have expected to find had she been on some type of drug. A little checking revealed that she was using the fen-phen combination.

Doctors were now on alert. There was a possibility that improper heart function could be an unknown side effect of the new diet pills. The doctors began to check other local hospitals for other patients with similar problems. They soon discovered thirty-three people taking this medication who had been admitted to hospitals with heart problems. Those who had undergone surgery had a shiny, white, waxy substance in their hearts.[9]

The doctors called the Federal Drug Administration (FDA), the government agency that regulates prescription medication. The FDA issued the following warning to doctors on July 8, 1997: "The popular diet-drug combination of fenfluramine and phentermine (fen-phen) might cause valvular heart disease in otherwise healthy women."[10]

According to *Time* magazine, "doctors realized that they had a potentially serious problem on their hands" because "more than 18 million prescriptions for these drugs were written" in 1996 alone.[11]

Several lawsuits have been filed on behalf of the users. According to *The Lancet*, these medications were approved by the FDA to be used separately, but not together.[12]

The *New England Journal of Medicine* published an article on the Mayo Clinic study. Editor Dr. Gregory Curfman released the results of the study before

Anyone who takes diet pills should be careful not to drink alcohol, smoke cigarettes, use products with caffeine in them, or take any other stimulants.

The fen-phen combination diet pills were found to cause heart problems in users. Many of those people were admitted to hospitals as a result of those problems.

publication, stating that "the public health significance is fairly immediate."[13]

On September 14, 1997, a new study discovered that 30 percent of 291 users of fen-phen were suffering from heart problems. The makers of these drugs have recalled all existing medication.[14]

Doctors have begun to prescribe the older amphetamine and methamphetamine diet pills once again. Despite their side effects, many people feel that they are the safest alternative. Other diet centers have begun urging their customer to use an antidepressant called Prozac™ with fenfluramine for weight control. Eli Lilly, the manufacturer of Prozac issued a warning stating that it disagreed with this idea. The practice "may be a significant public health risk." The makers of Prozac urged doctors and patients to use Prozac appropriately, for treatment of depression and not as a diet aid.[15]

As many as 58 million Americans are seriously overweight. (Someone who is seriously overweight is defined as being 20 percent or more overweight.) And the number of overweight people in this country—both young and old—continues to grow.[16] There are no simple solutions.

five

Treatment Programs That Work

There are treatment programs that specialize in helping people who have weight problems. There are also programs that specialize in treating people who are bulimic. Others are for those who have problems with anorexia. Still others treat people who have become addicted to diet pills. Each of these programs is designed to treat specific problems. The type of treatment a person needs will be determined by the type of problem he or she has. Let's take a closer look.

Treatment Programs That Focus on Addiction

Some people need help because they have become addicted to diet pills. Drug counselors can help. They can be found in the yellow pages of the phone directory under the headings of "Drug

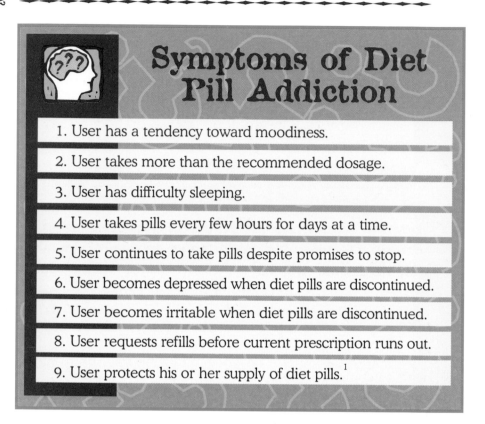

Symptoms of Diet Pill Addiction

1. User has a tendency toward moodiness.

2. User takes more than the recommended dosage.

3. User has difficulty sleeping.

4. User takes pills every few hours for days at a time.

5. User continues to take pills despite promises to stop.

6. User becomes depressed when diet pills are discontinued.

7. User becomes irritable when diet pills are discontinued.

8. User requests refills before current prescription runs out.

9. User protects his or her supply of diet pills.[1]

Counselors," "Drug Treatment Centers," "Addiction Counselors," or "Alcohol and Drug Counselors."

A counselor who has been trained to treat drug addiction will be the most helpful. Some counselors have letters like "CADC" after their name. This stands for Certified Alcohol and Drug Counselor. Others may have "MAC" after their name. This stands for Master Addiction Counselor. Some may have "ICADC" after their name. This stands for International Certified Alcohol and Drug Counselor. These counselors have been through training and have met state, national, or international standards.[2] They are the real experts and will be able to treat people who are addicted.

Treatment Programs That Focus on Anorexia

When people become so obsessed with their weight that they have been limiting their food intake for several months or longer, they may have a disease known as anorexia nervosa. In addition to severely starving themselves, anorectics may exercise excessively and abuse diet pills.

People with this problem see themselves as grossly overweight when they are actually starving themselves. They may be so malnourished that their lives are being seriously threatened. As a result, about one in ten people with this disorder will die.

Their friends and family will see them getting thinner and will often point out that they look terrible. The

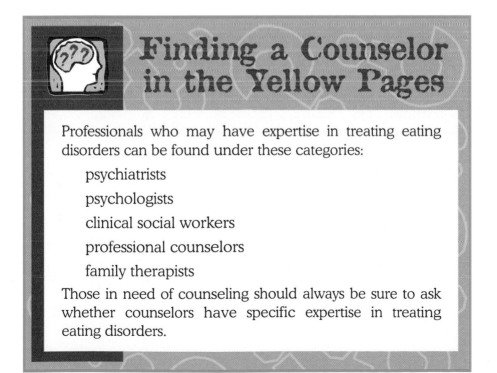

Finding a Counselor in the Yellow Pages

Professionals who may have expertise in treating eating disorders can be found under these categories:

psychiatrists

psychologists

clinical social workers

professional counselors

family therapists

Those in need of counseling should always be sure to ask whether counselors have specific expertise in treating eating disorders.

anorectic will not accept their opinions and will continue to focus on losing weight. Dieting may become so severe that their brain and other essential organs will be damaged from lack of nutrition.[3]

Some doctors specialize in treating anorexia nervosa—generally, medical doctors (M.D.s) or doctors of osteopathy (D.O.s). About half of all anorectics must be hospitalized in order to survive.[4]

Treatment Centers That Focus on Bulimia

Most people think of bulimics as people who eat and then throw up. This process is called binging and purging. Actually, bulimics are people who eat excessive amounts of food, then try to rid their bodies of it before they gain weight. They may do this in several ways. Some bulimics may use laxatives. Others use diuretics (water pills). Still others may abuse diet pills.

Bulimics usually don't become addicted to diet pills, because their excessive eating episodes are relatively infrequent, and they tend to use a variety of strategies to deal with the consequences. Strategies include excessive exercise, vomiting, use of laxatives and diet pills. People have had heart attacks and strokes from abusing diet pills.

Even if a bulimic does not use diet pills very often, repeated vomiting can cause serious health problems. The stomach acid that is vomited is stronger than the acid in batteries. With repeated exposure, vomit can eat holes in the esophagus (throat). Also, the person could also accidentally inhale the vomit. This could damage the lining of the lungs, causing breathing problems for the rest of the person's life. Every year a few bulimics actually inhale so much of their stomach's contents that they drown in their own vomit.[5]

Exercise, when done in moderation, is an excellent way to keep in shape physically and mentally.

Some bulimics abuse diuretics (water pills). This practice can be dangerous. They could be damaging their kidneys with every use. This can make their kidneys less capable of functioning properly. The kidneys eventually become so damaged that they will not clear water and wastes from the body. As a result, the legs, ankles, and feet will swell. Even worse, uric acid will accumulate in the body and could reach toxic levels. In other words, the body may slowly poison itself.

Treatment Centers That Focus on Obesity

Many people who use diet pills do so because they have a weight problem. Abusing diet pills is not the answer, however. A thorough evaluation by a doctor to find out why someone is overweight is the first step toward finding a solution. There are numerous possibilities.

A thyroid problem is one possible reason for weight gain. The thyroid gland is a very small organ located in the neck. If it is underactive, weight gain will occur until the thyroid problem is corrected. Usually thyroid medication is prescribed.

Some people may be genetically at risk to be overweight. If this is the case, diet pills may not be the solution. A doctor could provide a reasonable diet and exercise program.

Other people may have a metabolism problem. Their bodies just do not burn calories very fast. There are medications designed to treat that problem. Others may have a problem with a specific body area. In this case, a doctor can advise a course of action.

Treatment Centers That Focus on Compulsive Overeating

Some people eat compulsively. That is, they eat because they are stressed out, worried, or depressed—not because they are hungry. Most diet pills are stimulants. They increase the level of stress in the body. If a person is already worried, they may actually gain weight by using diet pills.

A smarter solution would be to see a counselor, get to the bottom of the stress, and find a healthier way to deal with it.

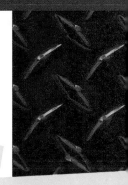

six

What You Can Do

There are a number of ways to get involved in activities that will promote self-esteem and encourage weight loss and control. They include developing a personal drug-free lifestyle, seeking treatment if there is a problem, encouraging others, and getting involved in an existing prevention project.

Developing a New Lifestyle

Unless someone is taking medicine under a doctor's supervision, it is important to develop a method for living without drugs. In order to do this, other ways of dealing with problems must be found. This includes weight problems. Most of the time diet pills do not lead to permanent weight loss. They may help in the initial weight loss process, but the weight usually comes right back

Regular exercise and a sensible diet (low in fat and calories) are the only proven effective and healthy ways to maintain weight loss permanently.

when someone stops taking the pills. In addition, diet pills usually cannot be taken for more than twelve weeks at a time.

Dr. Randy Eischner is a medical columnist for the *Daily Oklahoman*. He said that "the greatest magic pill in the world is you!"[1] By this, he meant that the key to weight loss is changing lifestyle. Decreasing the amount of fat and calories and increasing the amount of exercise will cause permanent weight loss.

Encouraging Others

Being a friend to others is helpful. If a student is being put down or abused by others because of his or her weight, being there is helpful. Encouraging people to live a healthy lifestyle, free of drugs, with a good diet and exercise routine, may help them to achieve their goals.

Avoid Peer Pressure

Peer pressure can be very hard to resist. But some of the biggest problems can start because of giving in to something inappropriate—simply because others are doing it. Learning to resist this pressure can be very important.

Getting Involved in a Drug Prevention Project

There are quite a few very effective prevention programs around. The biggest problem may be finding the right one. That is because there are so many of them, and they all have different names. Let's take a closer look at a few of them.

Athletes Coaching Teens (ACT)

The Athletes Coaching Teens (ACT) program is being used in the Richmond, Virginia, school system.[2] This program uses professional, college, and high school athletes to talk to middle school students. The program uses athletes because many middle school students look up to them.

Topics addressed include

1. Turning dreams into personal goals.
2. Developing a plan to reach these goals.
3. Identifying roadblocks like peer pressure and drug use.
4. Using problem-solving skills to overcome roadblocks.
5. Using techniques to increase self-esteem.

Friendly PeerSuation

The Friendly PeerSuation program is a project of the Girls Clubs of America.[3] It is currently in use in five communities around the country: Arlington, Texas; Birmingham, Alabama; Pinellas County, Florida; Rapid City, South Dakota; and Worcester, Massachusetts. However, it is expected to be introduced in over 240 locations during the next few years.

The program works like this: Older teens (called "PeerSuaders") are taught about community resources, goal setting, refusal skills, and problem solving. They are then matched up with younger teens (called "PeerSuade-Mes"). The PeerSuaders then work with groups of up to ten PeerSuade-Mes to teach them these skills in a positive, helpful environment.

Professional, college, and high school athletes in the ACT program talk to students about positive methods for dealing with peer pressure and for setting and reaching goals.

Young people helping other young people are an excellent source of information and support in times of crisis.

Lakeview Substance Abuse Prevention Project (LSAPP)

The Lakeview Substance Abuse Prevention Project (LSAPP) is located in Lakeview, Illinois.[4] It is run by six community agencies, which are cooperating in an attempt to provide drug prevention. The agencies are Youth Outreach Services (YOS), Neon Center for Youth (NCY), the Northside Ecumenical Night Ministry (NENM), Transitional Living Programs (TLP), Gateway Foundation (GF), and the Counseling Center of Lakeview (CCL).

YOS provides prevention programs in the eleven Lakeview high schools. NCY trains youth volunteers to provide prevention presentations to youth. NENM sends ministry members into nightspots frequented by youth to provide a trusted presence. TLP has a twenty-four-hour crisis line, emergency shelter, and referral services for youth. GF provides prevention programs to middle and high schools and counseling to students. CCL does case management and follow up services for adolescents and their families. There are opportunities for youth involvement at each of these agencies.

There are even prevention programs that focus on various cultural populations, for example, Hispanic Americans.

National Council of La Raza (NCLR)

The National Council of La Raza (NCLR) is the largest culture-specific prevention program in the United States.[5] NCLR has numerous prevention and empowerment programs. There are many more such opportunities for involvement.

questions for discussion

1. What would you say to someone who is thinking of using someone else's diet pills?

2. Is there ever a good reason to use diet pills?

3. What would you do if you knew that other students were calling someone names because of that person's appearance?

4. What would you say to someone who was eating and then purposely vomiting?

5. Would you tell anyone if you believed that a friend was anorectic?

6. Is there anything that can be done to help a compulsive overeater?

7. Why do you think some people can eat more than others without gaining weight?

8. What advice would you give to someone who seemed to be exercising too much?

9. If a person couldn't stop using diet pills, what advice would you give them?

10. What could your school do to help people who are worried about their weight?

11. What could you do to help people feel as if they "fit in"?

12. What is the single, most important thing you learned from reading this book?

chapter notes

Chapter 1. Diet Pills: New Questions, Same Answers

1. Author interview with "Jean," October 4, 1997.

2. Kim Flodin, "Bitter Pills: Teens and Appetite Suppressants," *American Health*, July/August 1991, p. 28.

3. Sue Kuba and Kimberly Allen, "Eating Disorders: The Hidden Impact," *EAP Digest*, 1988, pp. 35–40.

Chapter 2. Teens and Self-Image

1. Author interview with "Alexandria," February 14, 1997.

2. Tamara Hill, "How I Lost 100 Pounds," *McCall's*, October 1997, p. 86.

3. Carla Rohlfing, "Get Fit, Fight Fat," *Family Circle*, October 7, 1997, p. 108.

4. Laura White, "10 Minutes to Slim Hips, Thin Thighs, Flat Tummy," *Cosmopolitan*, October 7, 1997, p. 130.

5. "I Just Want to Be Pretty," *The Sally Jessie Raphael Show*, September 19, 1997.

6. Nancy Friday's comments from "I Just Want to Be Pretty," *The Sally Jessie Raphael Show*, September 19, 1997.

7. Sabina Solin, "I Was Dying to Be Thin," *Seventeen*, November 1995, pp. 124–129.

8. Ibid.

9. Performance Resource Press, *Eating Disorders* (Troy, Mich.: Performance Resource Press, Inc. undated), pp. 1–2.

10. Author interview with "Emilee," September 14, 1997.

11. Performance Resource Press, pp. 1–2.

12. Leslie Lompert, "Are You Obsessed With Food?" *Ladies' Home Journal*, May 1997, pp. 88–96.

Chapter 3. Confessions of a Diet Pill Addict

1. Author interview. Subject's name is omitted by request, September 11, 1997.

Chapter 4. How Diet Pills Work

1. *Confusion About Alcohol and Other Drugs* (Jackson, Mich.: National Safety Council, 1991), p. 26.

2. *Physicians' Desk Reference* (Oradell, New Jersey: Charles Baker, 1997), pp. 1289–1290.

3. Ibid.

4. "Phentermine," *Medical Drug Reference 2.0 for Windows*, 1994–1995, p. 1.

5. Christine Gorman, "Danger in Diet Pills?" *Time*, July 21, 1997, p. 58.

6. Maureen Conally, "The Better Way: The New (Doctor Approved) Diet Pills," *Good Housekeeping*, June 1996, pp. 141–142.

7. Jane Clark, "Could This Pill Be What You're Hungry For?" *Kiplinger's*, November 1996, p. 108.

8. Jamie Reno, "Weighty Problems," *Newsweek*, July 21, 1997, p. 65.

9. Alicia Ault, "FDA Issues Warning on Diet-Drug Combination," *The Lancet*, July 19, 1997, p. 189.

10. Ibid.

11. Christine Gorman, "Danger in Diet Pills?" *Time*, July 21, 1997, p. 58.

12. Ault, p. 189.

13. Gregory Curfman, "Diet Pills–Redux," *New England Journal of Medicine*, August 28, 1997, pp. 629–630.

14. Michael Lemonnick, "The Mood Molecule," *Time*, September 29, 1997, pp. 77–82.

15. Ibid.

16. Rita Losee, "Obesity: An EAP Concern," *EAP Digest*, March/April 1988, pp. 43–46.

Chapter 5. Treatment Programs That Work

1. "Phentermine," *Medical Drug Reference 2.0 for Windows*, Parsons Technology, 1994–1995, p. 1.

2. *Role Delineation Study for Alcohol and Other Drug Abuse Counselors* (Richmond, Va.: Columbia Assessment Services, 1991), p. 4.

3. Sabina Solin, "I Was Dying to Be Thin," *Seventeen*, November 1995, pp. 124–129.

4. Kelly Brownell and John Foreyt, *Handbook of Eating Disorders* (New York: Basic Books, 1986), p. 272.

5. Ibid., p. 301.

Chapter 6. What You Can Do

1. Randy Eischener, "A Healthy You," *The Daily Oklahoman*, September 22, 1997, p. 26.

2. Albert Farrell et al., "Athletes Coaching Teens for Substance Abuse Prevention," *Working With Youth in High-Risk Environments* (Rockville, Md.: Office of Substance Abuse Prevention, 1992), pp. 13–30.

3. Delores Wisdom, "A Profile of High-Risk Young Women in the Girls Clubs of America's Friendly PeerSuation Project," *Working With Youth in High-Risk Environments* (Rockville, Md.: Office of Substance Abuse Prevention, 1992), pp. 55–58.

4. William Southwick and Sharon Zahorodnyj, "Characteristics of Youth Women in High-Risk Environments," *Working With Youth in High-Risk Environments* (Rockville, Md.: Office of Substance Abuse Prevention, 1992), pp. 43–49.

5. "Empowering Hispanics," *The Prevention Pipeline* (Rockville, Md.: Center for Substance Abuse Prevention, 1993), pp. 16–19.

where to write

American Anorexia/Bulimia Association
265 W. 46th Street
Suite 1108
New York, NY 10036
212-575-6200
<http://members.aol.com/amanbu/>

American Council for Drug Education
204 Monroe Street
Rockville, MD 20852
1-800-488-DRUG (3784)
<http://www.acde.org/>

**National Association of Alcoholism
and Drug Abuse Counselors**
1911 North Fort Myer Drive, Suite 900
Arlington, VA 22209
703-741-7686
<http://www.naadac.org/>

**National Association of Anorexia
& Associated Disorders**
P.O. Box 7
Highland Park, IL 60035
847-831-3438

**National Clearinghouse for Alcohol
and Drug Information**
P. O. Box 2345
Rockville MD 20847
800-729-6686
<http://www.health.org/>

National Families in Action
2957 Clairmont Road, Suite 150
Atlanta, GA 30329
404-248-9676
<http://www.emory.edu/NFIA/>

National Family Partnership
8730 Georgia Avenue
St. Louis, MO 63105
314-845-1933
<http://www.nfp.org/help.html>

Overeaters Anonymous World Service Office
P. O. Box 44020
Rio Rancho, NM 87174-4020
505-891-2664
<http://www.overeatersanonymous.org/>

**PRIDE (Parents' Resource Institute
for Drug Education)**
3610 De Kalb Technology Pkwy.
Atlanta, GA 30340
770-458-9900
<http://www.prideusa.org/>

Weight-Control Information Network
1 Win Way
Bethesda, MD 20892
800-946-8098

further reading

Bergman, Yolanda, and Daryn Eller. *Food Cop*. New York: Bantam Books, 1991.

Bricklin, Mark, and Linda Konner. *Your Perfect Weight*. Emmaus, Pa.: Rodale Press, 1995.

Cash, Thomas. *The Body Image Workbook*. Oakland, Calif.: New Harbinger Publications, 1997.

Clayton, Lawrence. *Amphetamines and Other Stimulants*. New York: Rosen Publishing, 1994.

Cypert, Samuel. *The Power of Self-Esteem*. New York: Amacon, 1994.

Field, Linda. *Creating Self-Esteem*. Rockport, Mass.: Element Books, 1993.

———. *Self-Esteem for Women*. Rockport, Mass.: Element Books, 1997.

Groger, Molly. *Eating Awareness Guide*. New York: Fireside Press, 1992.

Kubersky, Rachel. *Eating Disorders: Anorexia and Bulimia*. New York: Rosen Publishing, 1992.

Levine, Suzanne. *50 Ways to Ease Food Pain*. Lynchwood, Ill.: Publications International, 1994.

Oxford, Jim. *Excessive Appetites*. New York: John Wiley and Sons, 1985.

Rapp, Robert. *The Pill Book Guide to Over-the-Counter Medications*. New York: Bantam Books, 1997.

Roth, Geneen. *Breaking Free from Compulsive Overeating*. New York: New American Library, 1984.

Rowland, Cynthia. *The Monster Within: Overcoming Bulimia*. Grand Rapids, Mich.: Baker Books, 1984.

Internet Addresses

Eating Disorders

<http://www.usd.edu/~pwyss/eat.dis.html>

<http://www.uihc.uiowa.edu>

<http://www.javanet.com/~jfutter/anorexia.htm>

<http://www.ndmda.org/eating.htm>

index

about the author

Lawrence Clayton, Ph.D., is a pastoral counselor who has spent the past twenty-five years working with children, young people, and families who have problems with alcohol and other drugs. He was the 1994 Oklahoma Alcohol and Drug Counselor of the Year and is the past president of the Oklahoma Drug and Alcohol Professional Counselor Certification Board. Dr. Clayton lives in the Midwest with his wife and their two teenagers.